WELCOME TO GLASGOW CATHEDRAL

The great cathedral of Glasgow stands majestically in the heart of Scotland's largest city. The awe-inspiring edifice is dedicated to St Kentigern, or St Mungo as he is affectionately known, the first bishop of the ancient British kingdom of Strathclyde, who was widely believed to have been buried on the site around 612.

The need to provide a more appropriate shrine to St Kentigern, for the use of pilgrims visiting his tomb, was the spur to building the present cathedral. Around it lay the chanonry, the precinct where the bishops (and later archbishops) and clergy had their residences. Between the cathedral and the River Clyde to its south, the thriving burgh of Glasgow sprang up, under the patronage of the bishop. The growth of the Merchant City since medieval times means that the cathedral is no longer physically at its centre – but without the cathedral there would be no city.

Above: St Kentigern, as represented in stained glass in a window of the choir.

Opposite: The west processional entrance.

CONTENTS

EXTERIOR FEATURES

6 THE TOWER AND SPIRE

Rebuilt following a lightning strike around 1406, the elegantly proportioned tower and spire once dominated the city.

7 THE PROCESSIONAL ENTRANCE

Beautifully moulded and surmounted by a huge traceried window, the western entrance was reserved for use on feast-days.

8 THE BLACADER AISLE

Built as an undercroft around 1250 and roofed by Archbishop Blacader around 1500, this extension forms an attractive side chapel.

INTERIOR FEATURES

12 THE PULPITUM

A decorative barrier designed to separate the nave from the choir, featuring a wealth of elaborate stone carving.

14 THE HIGH ALTAR

The central focus of the upper church, where St Kentigern's would once have stood.

16 THE TOMB OF ST KENTIGERN

The cathedral's spiritual heart in the crypt, where countless pilgrims sought blessing from the relics of the saint.

GLASGOW CATHEDRAL AT A GLANCE

Glasgow Cathedral is one of the outstanding architectural glories of Scotland's 'Golden Age' in the 13th century. The 16th-century Protestant Reformation and the 18th-century Industrial Revolution have taken their toll on the building, yet it remains the only medieval cathedral on the Scottish mainland to survive virtually complete. Its vast scale and fine detailing testify to the strength of belief and the power and wealth of the Church in the High Middle Ages.

The intention of the builders was threefold: to create an eye-catching structure that would dominate the landscape for miles around; to provide a stunning interior space in which the clergy could maintain the daily round of services; and to establish a fitting pilgrim route to the relics and tomb of St Kentigern. The names of those who created this masterpiece are unknown to us, but the fruits of their labour – the spacious elegance of the choir and presbytery, the bewitching gloom of the crypt beneath, and soaring over all the slender spire – stand as silent witness to their faith, their skills and their art.

Opposite: A 19th-century view of the cathedral from the NE, with the Molendinar Burn in the foreground.

DISTINCTIVE DETAILS

7 WINDOWS
There are well over a hundred in the building, in a variety of styles.

13 STAINED GLASS
One of the cathedral's most dazzling features, in a wide variety of styles, including rare Munich Glass above the crossing.

19 CEILING BOSSES
Among the cathedral's most attractive decorative features. Locations include the choir, the Blacader aisle, the chapter houses and the crypt.

AMBITIOUS BISHOPS

23/24 BISHOP JOCELIN
Jocelin (1175–99) launched a scheme to enlarge the cathedral, and commissioned a biography of St Kentigern.

24 BISHOP BONDINGTON
Bondington (1233–58) greatly enlarged the cathedral, bringing it close to the form we see today.

29 BISHOP WISHART
Wishart (1271–1316) encouraged Robert Bruce to seize the crown and drive out the English.

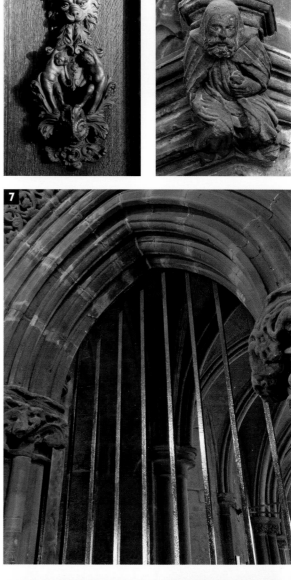

A SHORT TOUR OF GLASGOW CATHEDRAL

This tour guides visitors around the cathedral, beginning with the exterior, and culminating in the crypt.

The cathedral has a somewhat unusual layout. The main body is divided into two roughly equal halves by transepts (cross-arms) that do not project beyond the width of the building. The eastern half housed the choir and presbytery, for the exclusive use of the bishop and clergy; but it also provided access for pilgrims visiting the shrine of St Kentigern at the eastern end. Beneath the choir (or quire) is the lower church, or crypt, housing St Kentigern's tomb and the Lady Chapel. The western half of the cathedral was the nave, where the lay people worshipped. A number of lesser structures project from the main rectangle, notably the Blacader aisle and the two-storey chapter-house block.

Key

1 West processional door
2 South door
3 Nave
4 Tower and spire
5 Pulpitum and crossing
6 Choir and presbytery (ground floor)
   Crypt (lower floor)
7 Chapter houses
8 Blacader aisle
9 Treasury

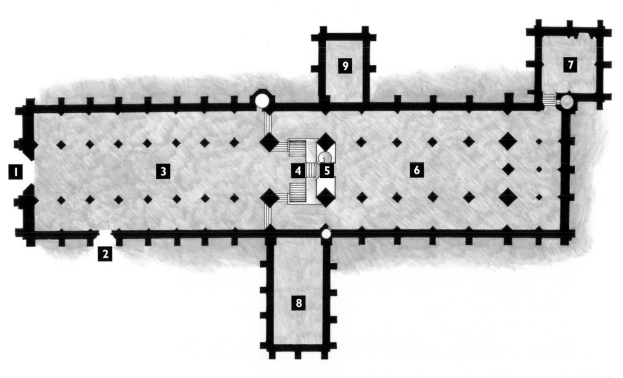

THE EXTERIOR

Much of the cathedral is of 13th-century date, with notable exceptions. These include the splendid central tower and spire, and the upper part of the chapter-house block at the NE corner, both rebuilt after a lightning strike around 1406.

The Blacader aisle projecting from the centre of the south side was completed by Archbishop Blacader (or Blackadder, 1483–1508). The aisle ends flanking the great west door date to the mid-1800s. They were added following the demolition of the two west towers.

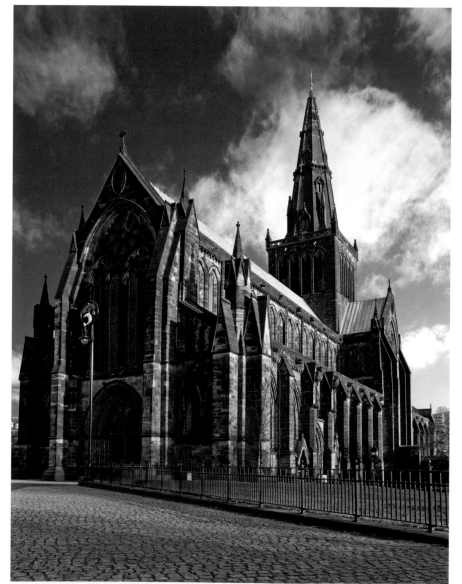

Top: One of the many gargoyles adorning the nave.

Above: The south transept.

Left: The cathedral from the SW.

THE WINDOWS

The cathedral has tiers of elaborate windows. There are well over a hundred of them, in a variety of shapes and sizes. The simplest windows have single pointed openings, known as lancets. There are also paired lancets (**1**), set either side-by-side or within surrounding arches. These are normally to be found in the lower walls, and are therefore among the earliest masonry, dating from the early 1200s.

At the next stage of complexity are groups of lancets with additional openings at their heads piercing arched plates of stone (**2**). This design is known as plate-tracery. These windows are generally higher up, and date from the mid-1200s. The windows lighting the choir aisles are among the most extraordinary and inventive examples of three-light plate-tracery anywhere in Britain.

There are also more complex windows featuring bar-tracery, in which the tracery patterns are defined by curved bars of stone (**3**). They date from the closing stages of the building programme in the later 1200s. Also dating from this period are the pairs of Y-traceried windows lighting the clearstory (top level) of the nave.

THE ENTRANCES

The cathedral originally had four entrances. The most imposing was the great processional west door. This was only used on certain days in the year, such as St Kentigern's feast day (13 January), and then by important visitors only. It is deeply recessed within a richly moulded frame, and divided into two openings by a central pier. Above it soars a fine, four-light, bar-traceried window. Both probably date from around 1270. The south door (through which visitors now enter the cathedral) was the normal entrance for the laity in medieval times. It has a handsomely moulded doorway with circular window above, featuring six trefoils (three arcs arranged in a circle). The two doors near the eastern end of the cathedral gave access into the crypt.

THE PROJECTING STRUCTURES

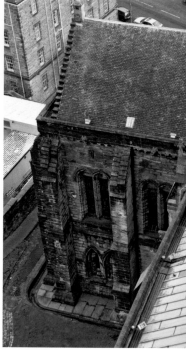

T hree structures project from the main body of the cathedral: the chapter houses at the NE corner, the treasury on the north side and the Blacader aisle on the south.

The chapter houses were meeting rooms for the chapter of senior clergy, who governed the cathedral. The two-storey chapter house building dates from the mid-1200s, though the upper floor was largely rebuilt after a lightning strike around 1406. The windows on this upper floor are subtly different, with plainer mouldings and lintelled openings within pointed arches.

The structure projecting halfway along the north side is the lower floor of a two-storey building. The missing upper storey was the sacristy, where the clergy prepared for services, and where their vestments

Above: The upper and lower chapter houses, viewed from the tower.

Top left: The treasury, formerly part of a two-storey building.

Bottom left: The Blacader aisle.

Below: A carved wyvern, one of several beasts that embellish the Blacader aisle.

and other items were stored. The lower storey was the treasury, where the cathedral's silver plate and other treasures were locked away. Now heavily restored, it was originally reached only by a stair down from the sacristy, for better security.

The structure projecting from the south side is the Blacader aisle. It was planned in the mid-1200s as a chapel accessed from the choir aisles, but only its crypt was completed. The unfinished structure was vaulted over around 1500 by Archbishop Blacader. His coat of arms appears on the central buttress of the south face. Carvings of uncertain date and meaning have been inserted between the windows, including Adam and Eve, a leopard, a camel, a dragon, a centaur, a unicorn and a wyvern (winged serpent).

Below left: The south wall of the choir, where the change in building styles is easiest to make out.

Bottom: The only bar-traceried window in the south wall of the choir, which was probably the last to be added.

LOOKING FOR BUILDING PHASES

Go to the south side of the eastern half. The rather squat third projecting buttress along from the Blacader aisle has a simple base course (a projecting moulding near the bottom). This dates from soon after 1200, when the transepts and nave were marked out on the ground. It runs westwards (left) from this point, across the transept (now hidden within the Blacader aisle) and around the south and north sides of the nave. The base course running eastwards (right) from this buttress, and all round the crypt, is more elaborate, and dates from the 1240s, when the present eastern arm of the edifice was begun.

THE TRADESMEN'S ENTRANCE

On the south side of the cathedral, to the right (east) of the Blacader aisle, is a four-light window with bar-tracery. It is different from its neighbours, which have only three lights and plate-tracery. This window was probably completed only when the choir was nearing completion in the 1260s. It may have been kept open to enable the builders to hoist materials up into the choir.

THE INTERIOR: THE NAVE

The nave was the part of the cathedral set aside for parish worship. This was also where the people of the diocese could gather on great festivals.

The main altars were at its east end, in front of the screens closing off the canons' choir beyond. There were eventually as many as 14 altars in the nave, many of which would have been in small, enclosed chapels within the flanking aisles or placed against the arcade piers. The altars were removed at the Reformation in 1560.

The nave is three storeys high. At the lowest level, arcades open into the stone-vaulted aisles to north and south. Above the arcades are galleries or triforia, with two sub-divided openings in each bay. At the top is the clearstory. A notable feature is the way the gallery and clearstory are interlinked by arches rising through both upper storeys, two to each bay. The roof dates to the early 20th century.

The nave has a tighter arcade rhythm than the choir, where the bays are considerably wider. This is because the nave's aisle walls were started soon after 1200, before the major change in plan around 1240. Much of the nave was built in the later 13th century, 60 years after the foundations had been laid.

Opposite: The three tiers of the nave.

Far left: The arcade at the lowest level of the nave.

Left: A 16th-century bell, recast in the 18th century, on display in the NW corner of the nave.

Above: Stained glass details from the top windows on the north side of the nave.

THE PULPITUM

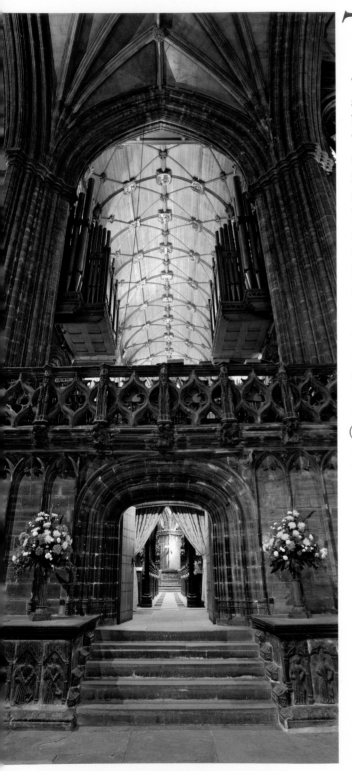

The east end of the nave is graced by an ornate stone pulpitum (screen), probably added in the early 1400s.

The pulpitum's central doorway is flanked by four arcaded panels. A traceried balustrade, punctuated by miniature buttresses, runs along the top. The base of the balustrade has a series of instructive carvings, possibly on the theme of marriage and fidelity. Patches of rough stone in the panels indicate the former position of projecting stone blocks that supported images. These corbels were removed when the altar platforms were placed in front of the screen. Archbishop Blacader's arms and initials appear on their sides. The north altar was dedicated to the Name of Jesus, and the south altar to Our Lady of Pity.

These altar platforms are a rare survival. They are decorated with low-relief figures, five on the north side, six on the south, within canopied recesses. These may be saints, though popular belief suggests that the 11 figures represent the faithful disciples (minus Judas Iscariot). The platforms were formerly connected to the flanking transepts by bridges. These were removed in 1855, when balustrades copied from the pulpitum were constructed above the symmetrical flights of stairs down to the crypt.

Left: Looking east through the pulpitum to the choir beyond.

THE TRANSEPTS AND CROSSING

The transepts and crossing are worth examining for the mixture of details which reflect those in the choir (of the mid–1200s) and the nave (later 1200s). On the west side of the crossing, the tower piers are like the nave piers, while those on the east side are like those of the choir. This indicates that when the choir was nearing completion, work continued into the transepts and nave, incorporating the parts started in the early 1200s. Construction of the transepts was possibly finished by 1277, when timber was obtained from Luss, in Dunbartonshire, for the bell tower and treasury.

Above left: The altar platforms at the foot of the pulpitum are carved with 11 figures thought to represent the faithful disciples of Christ.

Above: Carved figures at the base of the balustrade, possibly relating to a marital theme.

Below: One of two windows high up in the crossing where Munich Glass is still in place.

THE MUNICH GLASS

The stained glass high up in the windows of the transepts is a rare example of the cathedral's Munich Glass still in position. In the 1860s, the Royal Bavarian Stained Glass Works, based in Munich, was invited to supply the cathedral with a complete new set of windows, one of the largest public art commissions of the Victorian age. Most of their output, at home in Germany, was destroyed during the Second World War. Here at Glasgow, between the 1930s and the 1960s, almost all of the Munich Glass was removed – but why? Was it because of a change in taste, or poor performance of the very bright colours? Or was it perhaps a result of anti-German feeling after the two world wars?

THE CHOIR, PRESBYTERY AND FERETORY

The main level of the eastern arm was built in the mid-1200s. It accommodated the stalls of the cathedral clergy (in the choir), the high altar (in the presbytery), the shrine to St Kentigern (in the feretory, or shrine chapel) and at least four lesser altars at the far east end; these were dedicated to (from north to south): St Catherine (St Bride); St Martin; St James; and Sts Stephen and Laurence.

To meet all of these needs – and to provide adequate circulation – the choir, presbytery and feretory were given aisles along three sides. All these areas would have been enclosed by screens, mostly constructed of timber, with doorways at several points.

The impression on entering the choir through the pulpitum is sublime. It is not a large building by European standards, but it is a highly accomplished piece of design. The four long, slender lancets at the east end arrest the attention. Below them are two arcade arches, in front of which St Kentigern's shrine once stood. The high altar would have been more centrally placed, compared to the location of the present-day communion table.

The long side walls each have two pairs of triforium openings in each bay above the arcades, and at clearstory level there are triplets of openings. The quality of the stonework is as impressive as the design, particularly the foliage carving on the pier capitals. The ceiling dates only from 1912, but probably reflects its predecessor, built after the lightning strike of around 1406. It stands 22.5 metres (74ft) high.

THE UPPER CHAPTER HOUSE

The upper chapter house is entered from the NE corner of the cathedral. It was largely rebuilt after the lightning strike. Masonry from the original 13th-century room is visible in the vaulting over the small entrance vestibule. The rest is largely reconstruction under Bishops Cameron (1426–46) and Turnbull (1447–64). The former added the fireplace, while the arms of the latter are on the vaulting.

There are two oddities about the room. First, although this was the more important of the two chapter houses, it has the simpler entrance. And second, the base of the central pier does not entirely correspond with the form of the pier, suggesting a change of design in the course of the work.

Top: One of the carved bosses on the choir ceiling, some of which depict the miracles of Christ.

Above: The coat of arms of King James I. The arms of Scottish monarchs and bishops of Glasgow alternate at the base of the choir ceiling.

Left: The choir, presbytery and feretory, looking east through the pulpitum. The present communion table occupies the probable site of Kentigern's shrine.

Top: The doorway leading into the upper chapter house.

Above: Inside the upper chapter house.

THE CRYPT

The lower church, or crypt, was built in the mid-1200s, to provide a more appropriate setting for the tomb of St Kentigern. It also housed the Lady Chapel (dedicated to the Virgin Mary) and provided access to the lower chapter house.

On each side, arcades support the arcades in the choir above. However, two arches in the crypt correspond to each of the arches above. The lower headroom here would have made arches of the same width excessively squat. The arches separate the main space from the aisles surrounding it on three sides, and the row of four chapels at the east end.

The main space is ingeniously subdivided by the positioning of the piers and the patterns of the vaulting. This gives emphasis to the square space around the site of St Kentigern's tomb, near the centre, and the Lady Chapel, which occupies the full width to the east. The result is a triumph of spatial subtlety with few equals of this period. At the junctions of many of the vault ribs are bosses with foliage decoration; some also have human heads. The best work is the developed stiff-leaf carving on the capitals of the piers around the tomb itself.

Beyond the Lady Chapel, a flight of steps leads down to the four east chapels – dedicated (from north to south) to St Nicholas, Sts Peter and Paul, St Andrew and St John the Evangelist. On the low wall between the chapels of Sts Peter and Paul and St Andrew is the damaged effigy of a bishop in mass vestments, thought to be Robert Wishart (1277–1316) (see page 29). In the SE corner of the crypt is St Kentigern's Well, from which water was drawn for liturgical use. Also in that chapel is a display of carved stones, including possible fragments from the base of St Kentigern's shrine (see page 25), and a painted stone thought to come from the 12th-century cathedral.

Above: Carved masonry thought to have formed part of St Kentigern's shrine.

Opposite: The site of the tomb of St Kentigern.

Bottom left: The ornately carved piers and vaulted ceiling that helped focus attention on the tomb.

Bottom right: A piece of painted masonry from the 12th-century cathedral, now on display in the crypt.

THE LOWER CHAPTER HOUSE

In the NE corner of the crypt is a fine doorway leading into the lower chapter house.

Carved on the left side of the doorway is a figure of Christ giving his blessing, with what appears to be a seated figure beneath it, and yet another figure at the base. These may represent a 'tree of Jesse', showing the ancestry of Christ. On the other side, the carvings terminate with a splendid dragon amid luxuriant foliage.

The chapter house vault, partly rebuilt after the lightning strike of around 1406, is carried on a central pier. On the vault bosses are the arms of Bishop Cameron, Queen Joan, James I's widow (died 1445), and the 5th Earl of Douglas (died 1439). On the dean's seat against the east wall, a Latin inscription informs us that the chapter house was refounded by Bishop Lauder (1408–26).

Above: A detail from the carved archway leading into the lower chapter house.

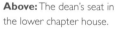

Above: The dean's seat in the lower chapter house.

THE OLDEST PART OF THE CATHEDRAL

Hidden away in the SW corner of the crypt is the oldest part of the cathedral. It probably dates from Bishop Jocelin's time (1174–99) and consists of a fragment of wall with a vertical engaged shaft (a pillar embedded in the wall). The feature may be a remnant of a symmetrical pair of small transepts flanking the site of Kentigern's tomb. The building of a new cathedral in the 1200s rendered these transepts obsolete. The change in style between the old and the new is most obvious in the capitals at the top of the shafts; the 12th-century capital has sprigs of stiff-leaf foliage, whereas the later capital beside it has plain horizontal mouldings.

Left: The engaged shaft which survives from the 12th-century cathedral.

THE BLACADER AISLE

The aisle was only intended as an undercroft to a main chapel on the upper floor (never built). Nonetheless, its vaulted ceiling is exceptional, of the type known as tierceron.

The depiction of St Fergus on the vault web above the entrance, with the inscription 'THIS.IS.YE.ILE OF.CAR[?].FERGUS', suggests that the aisle was thought to be the burial place of this holy man. Kentigern is said to have followed Fergus's hearse from Carnock to Glasgow as a prelude to his missionary activity here. The aisle would have formed part of the pilgrim circuit within the cathedral.

Above: The Blacader aisle, whose ceiling was added around 1500 by Archbishop Blacader.

Right: Bosses from the vaulted ceiling. Archbishop Blacader's coat of arms is shown at the top; other bosses feature crowned heads, skulls, mythical beasts and floral designs.

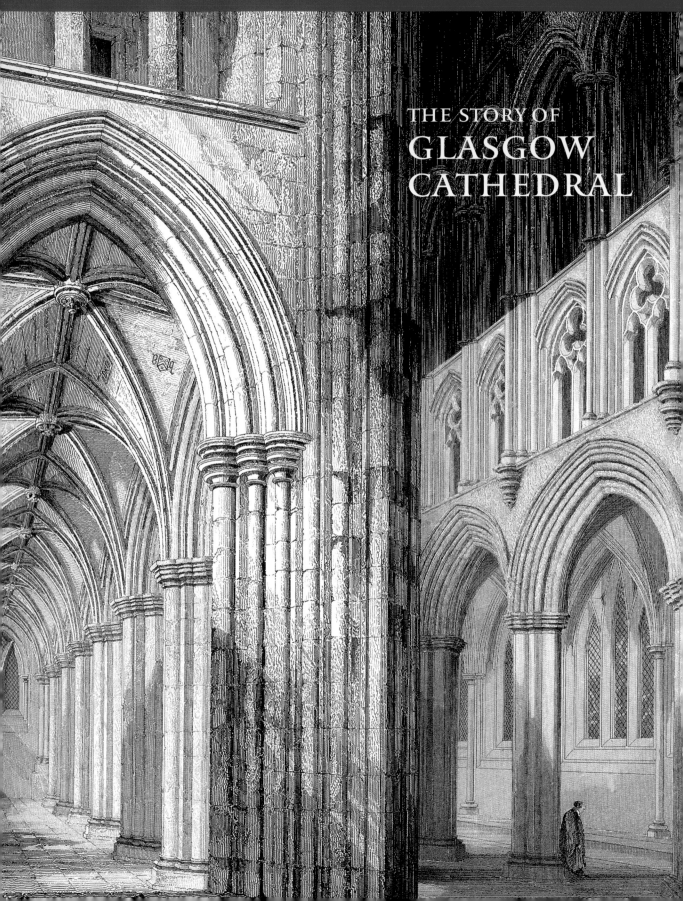

THE STORY OF
GLASGOW CATHEDRAL

Ｔhe history of Glasgow Cathedral is closely linked with the legend of St Kentigern, affectionately known as St Mungo. The name Kentigern (meaning 'hound-lord') is British in origin. His nickname, Mungo, probably meant 'dear beloved'.

Apart from a record of Kentigern's death around 612 in the *Welsh Annals*, all we know of him comes from two 12th-century biographies, and these are very unreliable. Tradition states that he was born at Culross, Fife. His mother, Thenew (also known as Enoch) had been cast adrift on the Forth by her father, King Loth (after whom Lothian may be named), as punishment for adultery. Kentigern was brought up in St Serf's monastery at Culross, before striking out on his own. He was led to Glasgow by an ox-drawn hearse carrying the body of another holy man, Fergus. Fergus's wish was to be buried in a cemetery reputed to have been consecrated by St Ninian.

No artefacts have been found at Glasgow Cathedral to corroborate such a tradition, although a human burial dated to between 687 and 781 was found in recent excavations. Some believe that Kentigern's first cathedral was at Govan, a little downriver on the other side of the Clyde, where large numbers of carved stones provide abundant evidence of an important ecclesiastical settlement. This was probably the dynastic burial place of the kings of Strathclyde, who ruled from Dumbarton Rock.

Putting aside such legends, what seems likely is that Kentigern founded a new church beside the Molendinar Burn in Glasgu, 'the green hollow'. He became bishop of a diocese that corresponded with the British kingdom of Strathclyde. This reached from Clach nam Breatann ('stone of the Britons') in the shadow of Ben Lomond in the north, to the Rere-cross, east of Penrith in Westmorland, NW England.

Top: A stained-glass representation of the young Kentigern with the fish that has become one of his symbols.

Above: The hearse of St Fergus, as depicted on the ceiling of the Blacader aisle, which once housed his shrine. Kentigern is said to have followed Fergus's body to Glasgow.

Opposite: The south aisle and nave dramatically rendered by R.W. Billings in 1847.

TIMELINE

MID-6TH CENTURY	612

KENTIGERN BORN possibly in Culross, Fife, where he is raised at St Serf's monastery and meets St Fergus.

DEATH OF KENTIGERN as recorded in the *Welsh Annals*. He is thought to be buried on the site of the cathedral.

BISHOP JOHN'S CATHEDRAL

Responsibility for establishing a defined diocese centred on Glasgow probably belongs to King David I, before he succeeded to the throne in 1124. His former tutor, John, was appointed between 1114 and 1118, and became the first bishop firmly associated with the diocese.

Named bishops had appeared in the records as early as the mid-11th century, but the first three – Magnus, John and Michael – seem to have been simply assistants of the archbishop of York. At that time, the archbishops of York claimed authority over the Scottish Church, and they were determined to maintain control of it.

Bishop John and King David struggled hard to resist the influence of York. Their bid to secure papal approval for a separate Scottish province, with an archbishop at St Andrews, proved unsuccessful during their lifetimes, but their efforts ultimately paid dividends. In 1175, Pope Alexander III recognised Glasgow as 'our special daughter, no-one in between', a status soon extended to the whole of the Scottish Church, except the diocese of Galloway.

Bishop John probably started building his cathedral soon after taking office. It was dedicated on 7 July 1136, though this may simply indicate that the building was sufficiently complete for services to be held therein. Nothing of his cathedral remains visible. However, excavations in 1992–3 located parts of what may have been the west front about one-third of the way down the present nave. Numerous pier stones, re-used in the walling of the next stage of building, may have come from John's cathedral.

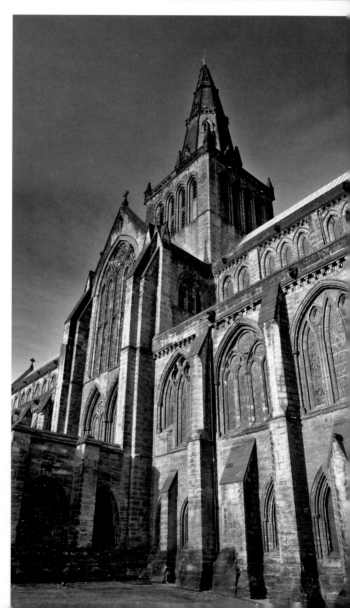

Right: The tower and spire seen from the SE.

Top right: David I (left) as depicted on the 12th-century charter of Kelso Abbey with his grandson, Malcolm IV.

THE DEATH OF SOMERLED AND THE CULT OF ST KENTIGERN

Bishop John's successor, Herbert (1147–64), commissioned the first of the two 12th-century biographies of Kentigern. Shortly before Herbert died, an event took place that considerably boosted St Kentigern's status.

That summer Somerled, the great 'King of the Isles', led a huge armada up the Clyde towards Glasgow in an attempt to seize the Scottish throne. On hearing the news, Herbert fervently prayed at Kentigern's tomb. The saint's body is said to have stirred, miraculously helping the men of Glasgow, under Walter Fitzalan the Steward, to defeat the men of the Isles. Somerled's severed head was brought from Renfrew to Glasgow. It was delivered to the cathedral, where the bishop declared, 'The Scottish saints are truly to be praised!' The event helped elevate St Kentigern in the national consciousness. A new biography of St Kentigern was commissioned by Bishop Jocelin, detailing the saint's miracles. Jocelin also set about enlarging his cathedral so that the cult of St Kentigern could be more properly accommodated.

Above left: Stained glass in a plate-traceried window on the south wall of the choir shows scenes from the life of St Kentigern.

Above: A detail from the same window shows a monk at work on Bishop Jocelin's biography of St Kentigern.

1136

GLASGOW CATHEDRAL is dedicated, though probably not completed.

1175

POPE ALEXANDER III recognises Glasgow as a 'special daughter, no-one in between'.

THE FIRST CATHEDRAL ENLARGED

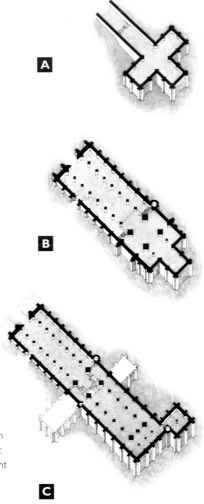

The *Melrose Chronicle* records that in 1181 Bishop Jocelin was 'gloriously enlarging' his cathedral at Glasgow.

His work was interrupted by a fire, but a second dedication was held on 6 July 1197. The only part of Jocelin's cathedral remaining visibly in place is the fragment of wall in the crypt (see page 18). The recent excavations also uncovered part of what may have been the north wall of the nave below the present nave arcading. Fragments of finely painted stonework found during the course of excavation may also have come from Jocelin's building.

BISHOP BONDINGTON'S NEW VISION

The radical decision to rebuild the cathedral to the form we now see was probably taken by Bishop William Bondington (1233–58). In Lent of 1242, the faithful throughout Scotland were urged to contribute to Bondington's new vision. The focus was to be centred on the eastern arm, which was to be almost as long as the nave, and with aisles not only along the north and south sides but across its east end also.

Right: Cutaway diagrams show how the cathedral is thought to have developed during the 12th and 13th centuries.
A The cruciform cathedral completed by Bishop Jocelin in 1197.

B The planned enlargement begun soon after 1200, probably by Bishop Walter.
C The even more ambitious enlargement commissioned by Bishop Bondington around 1240.

GLASGOW FAIR

Glasgow Fair originated in the late 12th century when King William I (left) granted Bishop Jocelin the right to hold a fair, to begin annually on 6 July. This date was to mark the start of celebrations in honour of St Kentigern.

William attributed the birth of his only son, Alexander II, to the intercession of St Kentigern. He was well into his fifties and heirless and Jocelin, as Kentigern's successor, had blessed the marriage bed.

Incidentally, Alexander was named after Pope Alexander III, who had declared Glasgow a 'special daughter' of Rome. The fair is now fixed to the second fortnight of July.

In addition to the high altar, dedicated to St Kentigern, there were also to be altars within four chapels at the eastern end. Bishop Bondington was also probably motivated by the desire to have a shrine to St Kentigern at the main level, in addition to his tomb in the crypt below. (We know this from records of visits by Edward I of England in 1301, when he made offerings at both levels.) The shrine could have been placed directly over the tomb, in the centre of the choir. However, the choice of plan suggests that there was a feretory (shrine chapel) east of the high altar, within a separate enclosure, which pilgrims could reach via the aisles running round three sides of the main space.

1181–97	1242–58

BISHOP JOCELIN
'gloriously' enlarges the cathedral, though work is interrupted by fire.

BISHOP WILLIAM DE BONDINGTON
sponsors a major redevelopment of the cathedral, greatly expanding its eastern section and adding the chapter houses.

A PILGRIM'S PROGRESS

The decision to build the cathedral anew in the 13th century was in part taken to create a fitting pilgrim route to the shrine and tomb of St Kentigern.

Standing in the vast, echoing space of the nave, one can imagine the scene on one the busiest days in the cathedral's calendar, 13 January, the Feast of the Nativity of St Kentigern. A throng of pilgrims would crowd expectantly into the nave. All would be jostling for a place in the queue that would lead them down the nave, along the narrow aisles, past the canons' choir and high altar to the holy man's shrine beyond, where a sight, perhaps even a touch if one was lucky, might bring comfort, maybe even a cure, for some affliction or another. From there they would descend the cold stone stairs, via the shrine to St Fergus in the Blacader aisle, into the crypt, towards the candle flames flickering over and around the saint's tomb. All the while they would be conscious of the overpowering smell of incense, the monotonous, hypnotic chanting of the canons, the murmuring of their fellow pilgrims praying and – from on high – the great bells in the cathedral's towering spire ringing out across the city and the countryside beyond.

Perhaps the most famous pilgrim was Edward I of England, during his invasion of Scotland in 1301–2. Over the course of four days in late August 1301, the 'Hammer of the Scots' made offerings at the high altar, feretory and 'tomb in the vault'.

Below: Pilgrims cluster around the elaborately decorated shrine in the feretory, at the eastern end of the choir.

There is doubt, however, about the precise nature of the shrine in the feretory behind the high altar. Both Jocelin's enlargement of the first cathedral and Bishop Bondington's new cathedral were doubtless intended to house the enshrined relics of St Kentigern, translated (i.e., relocated) from their tomb in the crypt. However, neither prelate received the necessary papal authority to do so. (A later attempt, by Bishop Lauder in the early 15th century, also failed.) So there in the crypt St Kentigern remained. Which begs the question: just what was placed in the feretory behind the high altar?

The answer may well be depicted on the seal of the chapter of Glasgow, created around 1233. The obverse shows a church-like structure, with central tower and spire, standing on a pillared arcade of three arches: Bondington's proposed new cathedral. The reverse shows a table with three kneeling figures praying before it, identifiable as pilgrims from their hats. And on that table is a waist-up effigy of St Kentigern in the act of benediction, with the words, 'KENTEGERNE TVOS BENEDIC PATER ALME MINISTROS' ('Kentigern, dear father, bless thy servants'). In the absence of the holy man's relics, perhaps the feretory housed such a table, possibly of stone, at which pilgrims could pray and perhaps receive succour. The effigy itself may well have been taken in procession during the most important festivals.

Top left: The tomb of St Kentigern in the crypt, to which pilgrims would progress after visiting the shrine above.

Above: The obverse and reverse of the seal of the chapter of Glasgow, dating from around 1233.

1301

EDWARD I
of England makes a four-day pilgrimage to the cathedral, during his brutal invasion of Scotland.

1301

BOTHWELL CASTLE
falls to Edward I immediately after he leaves Glasgow to resume his conquest of Scotland.

BISHOP WISHART – THE BATTLING BISHOP

I n the crypt lies the headless stone effigy of a bishop. It is believed to represent one of the towering figures in Scotland's medieval history – Bishop Wishart.

Robert Wishart (1271–1316) was inevitably caught up in the catastrophic events that followed the death of seven-year-old Queen Margaret 'Maid of Norway' in 1290. During the process that resulted in John Balliol's enthronement in 1292, he supported the rival Bruce claim to the succession. With Wallace and others, he led the resistance to Edward I in 1297. For this he earned the undying hatred of the English king.

But Wishart's greatest moment in the resistance to English imperialism came in the spring of 1306, soon after Sir John Comyn's murder in the Greyfriars' Church, Dumfries, by Robert Bruce, grandson of Bruce 'the Competitor'. As Bruce hastened to Scone for his inauguration as king, he visited Glasgow to confer with Wishart, in whose diocese the murder had taken place. Far from excommunicating Bruce, Wishart urged him on. He gave him episcopal robes and vestments fit for a king, and a royal banner he had been hiding in his treasury for such a moment as this.

Despite his advancing years, Wishart threw his considerable weight behind the new king, exhorting his flock to crusade against the English. He even used timber given by Edward I to help repair the cathedral's bell-tower to make siege engines for use against the English garrison holed up in Kirkintilloch Castle! But the 'wicked bishop', as the English knew him, was captured soon afterwards in Cupar Castle, clapped in irons and taken to England. His clerical rank saved him from death; instead he was thrown into a Wessex dungeon. And there he languished until his repatriation after the Battle of Bannockburn in 1314. By now blind and old, he returned to his native land with his fellow prisoners, Bruce's queen, sister and daughter. He died on 26 November 1316 and was laid to rest in his beloved cathedral.

Above: The headless effigy of Bishop Wishart in the crypt.

Opposite: The great processional doors in the cathedral's west face.

1306

ROBERT BRUCE receives encouragement from Bishop Robert Wishart, despite murdering his rival, John Comyn, in a church. He seizes the throne, but Wishart is captured by the English.

1314

BISHOP ROBERT WISHART is released from English captivity, following Bruce's victory at Bannockburn.

THE LATER MIDDLE AGES

Following the completion of Bishop Bondington's cathedral, there was little reason for further building other than structural failure or the wish for liturgical changes.

For example, soon after 1400 the cathedral was struck by lightning, requiring the building of a new central tower and spire and the rebuilding of the upper chapter house. Bishop Lauder may also have taken the opportunity to erect the fine pulpitum. The building of the Blacader aisle is described on page 9.

At some stage two towers were added to the west front. The one at the NW corner appears to date from the late 13th century, and may therefore have been the steeple Bishop Wishart was reported to be building in 1277. The SW tower followed around a century later. We do not know what role was intended for these towers, except that the NW tower was used as a belfry. By 1400, though, the NW tower was serving as the consistory house, where the court administering ecclesiastic law sat, and the cathedral library. Both towers were demolished in the mid–19th century.

Opposite: A painting from the late 18th or early 19th century shows the NW tower at the far right. This was probably added by Bishop Wishart in the 1270s.

Above: One of the carved figures on the pulpitum, thought to have been installed when the new tower and spire were built in the early 15th century.

THE ARMS OF THE CITY OF GLASGOW

The city's coat of arms is inspired by some of the miracles associated with Kentigern. At the top is St Serf's pet robin, brought back to life by Kentigern after it had been killed by jealous schoolmates. At the bottom is a fish with a ring in its mouth. This refers to Kentigern's assistance to the penitent Queen Languoreth: she had given a ring to a lover which, when demanded by her husband, was found in the stomach of a fish caught by Kentigern's monks. The tree, from which hangs Kentigern's bell, refers to a fire which Kentigern started with one of its branches.

1406

A LIGHTNING STRIKE causes severe damage to the central tower, the spire and the upper chapter house.

1408

BISHOP WILLIAM LAUDER is appointed and soon begins repairing the tower and spire. His coat of arms is engraved on the parapet.

31

CASTLE, CHANONRY AND TOWN

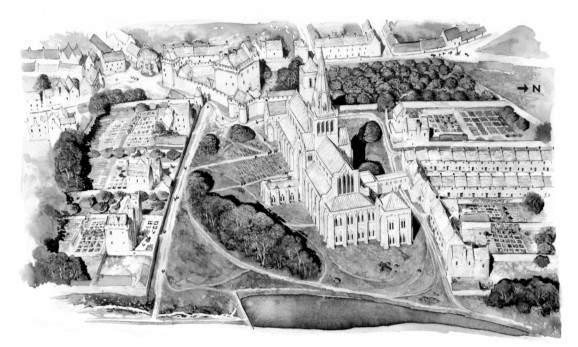

Glasgow's bishops and clergy all had residences in the chanonry, the precinct around the cathedral. Some of this accommodation was magnificent, but the quality of housing followed a strict hierarchy.

The most splendid residence was the bishop's castle. This was situated immediately west of the cathedral. It had extensive orchards to its north (on the site of the present Royal Infirmary). In its final state, the castle's main focus was a great tower house, built or extended by Bishop Cameron around 1430. Around it was a high curtain wall, with towers at one or more of the angles, rebuilt by Archbishop James Beaton (1503–23). His successor, Archbishop Dunbar (1523–47), erected an imposing gatehouse.

The manses of the dignitaries and canons were also substantial. Some had the appearance of small tower houses of three or more storeys; others were more urban in appearance, with just two storeys. The dean and treasurer lived south of the cathedral, the chancellor and chanter to the north. The only manse remaining is Provand's Lordship, west of the cathedral, which served the prebendary of Barlanark in the 16th century. The building, however, probably began life in the 15th century as part of the cathedral's hospital.

We know a little of the quality of life of the canons from an inventory of the possessions of Canon Adam Colquhoun, drawn up in 1542. The main rooms in his house were his hall, chamber, oratory and kitchen, with a

Above: A reconstruction drawing shows the cathedral chanonry in the later Middle Ages. The bishop's castle stands just west of the cathedral, while the terraced houses to the north were occupied by the vicars choral (see page 35).

Opposite top: Provand's Lordship, across the High Street from the cathedral, was probably part of a 15th-century hospital, but later became a manse for one of the canons.

Opposite centre: A heraldic panel from the bishop's castle (now the site of the St Mungo Museum) is on display in the crypt.

brewhouse, barn and stable attached. His lodgings were furnished with many costly items, some said to be of Flemish workmanship. Apparently he also had a mistress and two children!

Less spaciously provided for than Canon Colquhoun were the vicars choral (see page 35). These occupied a separate close of smaller manses north of the north transept. Each had a ground-floor hall and an upper chamber. The vicars also had use of a communal hall and kitchen, connected to the cathedral sacristy by a bridge.

Beyond the chanonry, a burgh grew up under the protection of the cathedral and its clergy. By the 1170s there was a market near the cathedral. But the area around the cathedral was not ideally suited to urban growth, and by the 13th century the nucleus of the burgh had shifted southward down the slope towards the Clyde. The cross of streets which developed at the point where the Molendinar Burn joined the Clyde became Trongate and Gallowgate (running east–west) and Saltmarket and High Street (north–south). By the mid-13th century, much of the land east of the High Street was occupied by the Dominican Friary (later taken over by the university, founded by Bishop William Turnbull in 1451), and in the later 15th century the ground on the other side of the street was given to the Franciscan friars.

In its prime, the great cathedral dominated the little town that sprouted up in its shadow. But with the coming of the 'Tobacco Lords' and the Industrial Revolution, the city expanded rapidly westward to form a new municipal and commercial heart, the Merchant City, around George Square. The cathedral's lofty steeple was left to vie with chimneys and cranes, and latterly tower blocks, for the skyline it once dominated. But although the cathedral today is no longer at the centre of the city, it remains a vital part of civic life, for without the cathedral there would be no city.

1430

BISHOP JOHN CAMERON builds or extends the great tower house of the bishop's palace.

1451

BISHOP WILLIAM TURNBULL founds the University of Glasgow.

THE CATHEDRAL CLERGY

The role of a medieval cathedral was very different from that of a modern church in a Protestant country. Like many other Scottish cathedrals, Glasgow served its local community as a parish church. But it was more important as the church within which the bishop of the diocese placed his cathedra or seat of office.

Services for the laity took place in the nave, but the worship that marked out cathedrals as different, and expressed their particular dignity, took place in the choir. These services consisted of a daily round of 'offices' modelled on monastic practice, in which the ordinary folk played little part. They were made up of psalms, readings, prayers and anthems. In addition, there were various celebrations of the mass, according to the particular importance of the day and the time of year.

A permanent staff of clergy, known as canons, ensured that the services were carried out properly. These canons formed a chapter, the body responsible for regulating the life of the cathedral and administering its possessions. They were also responsible for electing the bishops, at least in the earlier years. Initially, the canons were supported by a shared fund; David I, for example, donated all the fat from the slaughter of his animals in Teviotdale, as well as an eighth of the profits of justice from Cumbria. Eventually each canon had his own endowment, or prebend, most of which came from appropriating much of the income of one or more parish churches. By the 16th century, Glasgow had 32 canons, more than any other Scottish cathedral. They administered an enormous bishopric which stretched down to the border with England.

Top: A reconstruction drawing shows medieval canons celebrating high mass at Elgin Cathedral.

Right: The arms of Archbishop Blacader, carved into the south altar platform at the foot of the pulpitum.

Among the canons were dignitaries with special responsibilities. They included the dean (head of chapter), the precentor or chanter (responsible for the music), the chancellor (the businessman) and the treasurer. By the later Middle Ages, many canons were spending much of their time away from Glasgow on other business; indeed, some regarded their prebends as little more than a source of income. Even the dignitaries were not required to be resident for more than half the year. To ensure the continuity of services, all but two of the canons had to provide clergy to deputise for them – these were known as vicars choral. The two other canons had to provide a sacristan and six choir boys.

In addition to the canons, there were priests who met the needs of the lay people, particularly during pilgrimages, and others who were paid to sing masses for the souls of the dead. It was to provide for such soul masses that many of the altars in the cathedral were founded. Around 1263, for example, Walter of Moray, lord of Bothwell Castle, endowed the altar of St Catherine in the choir, adjacent to the upper chapter house, for the good of his soul and those of his forebears.

Top right: An illuminated page from Archbishop Blacader's prayer book, thought to show the owner praying at the feet of the crucified Christ.

DID YOU KNOW . . .

Even though Robert Blacader was Bishop of Glasgow, he had no place in the chapter. In 1487 he tried to find a way round the problem by acquiring a prebend but he still failed to become a member of the board!

ABOUT 1500

ARCHBISHOP ROBERT BLACADER

adds a vaulted ceiling to the 13th-century projection on the cathedral's south wall, now known as the Blacader aisle.

1557

ARCHBISHOP JAMES BEATON

appeals to the Earl of Arran for support in response to the gathering storm of the Reformation. To his dismay, the earl embraces Protestantism.

THE REFORMATION AND AFTER

The Protestant Reformation of 1560 marked the end of the mass and the rejection of papal authority, but the process of reform was protracted. Although Archbishop Beaton (1550–70) left for Paris in 1560, in 1572 it was said that only six of the prebendary canons had embraced Protestantism.

A separate chapter had to be formed to ensure that reformed archbishops were elected. Protestant ministers had to be provided by the burgh, which was allowed to tax the inhabitants to pay for them. By 1595 there were four of them in post.

The furnishings associated with Catholicism were immediately 'cleansed', but it seems the roof coverings were also removed, for in 1574 the town council had to take steps to reverse the decay. However, the survival of the cathedral during these dramatic years of change was ensured by its use as a Protestant building.

Three separate congregations now worshipped in it. The Inner High Kirk used the former choir and presbytery, the Outer High Kirk occupied the western part of the nave, and the Barony Kirk was established in the crypt. Confusingly, the transepts and east bays of the nave, which served as the vestibule to all three kirks, came to be known as 'The Choir'. Walls were eventually built between the various parts. The one at the west end of the choir was in place by 1635; and the one in the nave by 1647. To adapt the churches for reformed worship, with its emphasis on preaching the Word of God rather than the mass, galleries were inserted within the aisles.

Above: A statue of the reforming churchman John Knox towers over the cathedral from the summit of the Necropolis.

Opposite top: A late-18th-century painting shows members of the Glasgow Trades House defending the cathedral from vandalism in 1579.

Opposite below left: Worshippers file through the pulpitum into the Inner High Kirk following the partition of the cathedral into three separate churches.

Opposite below right: Stained-glass tributes to the Glasgow Trades, in the 'tradesmen's entrance' window of the choir (see page 9).

1560

THE REFORMATION establishes Protestantism as the official religion in Scotland, with John Knox (left) among its leaders. Archbishop Beaton flees to France.

1579

MEMBERS OF THE TRADES HOUSE defend the cathedral, allowing it to survive the Reformation relatively unscathed.

RESTORED TO FORMER GLORY

I n the early 19th century a growing appreciation of medieval architecture resulted in new attitudes towards the cathedral. There were calls for its restoration to former glory. Schemes were drawn up, and it wasn't long before 'restoration' was being put into effect.

Unfortunately the early attempts would be considered misguided by today's standards. In 1846 and 1848, for example, the two lop-sided west towers were demolished. The plan was to replace them with new towers, more symmetrical and more architecturally imposing, but funds were not forthcoming. Instead, the present rather unadventurous ends to the nave aisles were formed.

The cathedral's interior was also opened out. By 1835, both the Barony Kirk and the Outer High Kirk had moved elsewhere in the city, enabling the removal of the cross-walls forming the 'Choir'. In 1852, the galleries in the Inner High Kirk were removed. Shortly afterwards the entire building passed into State care. This was the long-deferred result of the Act of Annexation of 1587, and the final abolition of episcopacy within the established church in 1689, which declared that Scotland's cathedrals were Crown property. Archbishop John Paterson (1687–9) was the last in the long and distinguished line of bishops founded by St Kentigern a thousand years earlier.

'THE DEAR GREEN PLACE'

The fabric of the building is now maintained by Historic Scotland on behalf of the Scottish Government. However, the cathedral continues in use as a place of worship.

It is no longer strictly a cathedral in the sense of being a bishop's church, but the minister, kirk session and congregation for whom it is a spiritual home rightly regard it as much more than just the parish church for the part of Glasgow in which it happens to sit.

Indeed, it is the setting for religious, artistic and civic activities that make it the focus of a significant part of Glasgow's life. The city in its turn takes great pride in the building that is the single most impressive survivor of the age in which it was created.

Above: The coffin of Donald Dewar, the former First Minister, during a memorial service at the cathedral in October 2000.

Left: Rangers footballers attend a memorial service at the cathedral in January 1971, following the Ibrox disaster in which 66 spectators died.

Opposite: An architect's drawing dated 1827 shows a proposal for new towers at the west of the building. The 13th-century towers were demolished in the 1840s but were never replaced.

1689

ARCHBISHOP JOHN PATERSON
becomes the city's last archbishop as episcopacy in Scotland is abolished.

1846-8

THE WEST TOWERS
are demolished, but plans to replace them never see fruition.

Glasgow Cathedral is one of more than 50 Historic Scotland properties in the west of Scotland, a selection of which is shown below.

BOTHWELL CASTLE

One of Scotland's great medieval castles, Bothwell was ravaged during the Wars of Independence, but its mighty donjon tower still survives.

↗ In Uddingston, off the B7071

🕐 Open all year
Winter: closed Thu/Fri

📞 **01698 816 894**

🚗 Approx. **10 miles** from Glasgow Cathedral

£ P 🅿 🔢 🚻 🛈 🏮 🔭

CRAIGNETHAN CASTLE

Sir James Hamilton's 16th-century fortress–residence was a state-of-the-art domestic stronghold, surrounded by deep gorges and abundant forests.

↗ Five and a half miles NW of Lanark, off the A72

🕐 Open all year
Winter: open weekends only

📞 **01555 860 364**

🚗 Approx. **25 miles** from Glasgow Cathedral

£ P 🅿 🔢 🚻 🛈 🏮 🍴 🔭

DUMBARTON CASTLE

The ancient capital of Strathclyde became an important fortress for the Stewart monarchs and still commands superb views over the Clyde.

↗ In Dumbarton off the A82

🕐 Open all year
Winter: closed Thu/Fri

📞 **01389 732 167**

🚗 Approx. **25 miles** from Glasgow Cathedral

£ P 🅿 🔢 🚻 🛈 🏮 🔭

NEWARK CASTLE

Built in the later 15th century and remodelled a century later, Newark was transformed from medieval tower house to splendid Renaissance mansion.

↗ In Port Glasgow on the A8

🕐 Open summer only

📞 **01475 741 858**

🚗 Approx. **25 miles** from Glasgow Cathedral

£ P 🅿 🔢 🚻 🛈 🏮 ⊗

For more information on all Historic Scotland sites, visit **www.historic-scotland.gov.uk**
To order tickets and a wide range of gifts, visit **www.historic-scotland.gov.uk/shop**

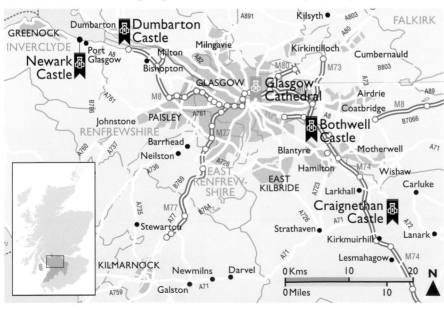

Key to facilities	
Admission charge	£
Bus/coach parking	🅿
Car parking	P
Interpretive display	🔢
Picnic area	🔢
Shop	🛈
Toilets	🚻
Self-serve tea and coffee	🍴
Bicycle rack	🚲
No dogs	⊗